Pratt

Booker T. Washington

A Photo-Illustrated Biography
by Margo McLoone

Reading Consultant
Dr. Gail Lowe
Anacostia Museum

Bridgestone Books
an Imprint of Capstone Press

Facts about Booker T. Washington

- Booker T. Washington was born a slave.

- The T in his name stands for Taliaferro.

- He started a school called Tuskegee Institute.

- He rode a horse around Tuskegee Institute every day.

Bridgestone Books are published by Capstone Press • 818 North Willow Street, Mankato, Minnesota 56001
Copyright © 1997 by Capstone Press • All rights reserved • Printed in the United States of America

Library of Congress Cataloging-in-Publication Data
McLoone, Margo.
    Booker T. Washington/by Margo McLoone.
p. cm.--(Read and discover photo-illustated biographies)
Summary: A brief biography of the man who was born a slave and worked in salt mines as a youth but went on to become a national leader for the education of African-Americans and founder of Tuskegee Institute.
    Includes bibliographical references and index.
    ISBN 1-56065-520-8
    1. Washington, Booker T., 1856-1915--Juvenile literature. 2. Afro-Americans--Biography--Juvenile literature. 3. Educators--United States--Biography--Juvenile literature. [1. Washington, Booker T., 1856-1915. 2. Educators. 3. Afro-Americans--Biography.]
I. Title. II. Series.
E185.97.W4M35   1997
970'.92--dc21   96-37381
[B]   CIP
                                                                               AC

Photo credits
Schomburg Center, cover, 8, 16
Bettmann Archive, 4, 10, 12, 14
Unicorn/Jeff Greenberg 6; Andre Jenny, 20
FPG, 18

Table of Contents

A Leading Educator

Booker T. Washington was an important educator. He started Tuskegee Institute in Alabama. It was a school for nonwhite students. He ran the school, taught classes, and raised money. He believed in schools that combined learning and work training.

Tuskegee became a well-known school. Students came from near and far to attend his school. Some teaching took place in the community, too. The school taught agriculture to local farmers. Agriculture is the science of farming.

Booker was also a national leader for African Americans. He spoke to large groups about his students' needs.

Booker felt that schools should combine learning and work training.

Early Life

Booker Taliaferro Washington was born in 1856 in Hales Ford, Virginia. He took his last name from his stepfather. His stepfather's name was Washington Ferguson.

Booker lived with his mother, Jane. She was a slave who cooked for a plantation owner. A slave is someone who is owned by someone else. A plantation is a large farm.

At age seven, Booker carried water to workers in the fields. He chased flies out of the dining room of the house. He carried sacks of corn to the mill on horseback.

In 1863, slaves were freed. Booker was nine years old. His family left the plantation. They moved to Malden, West Virginia, to find work.

Booker lived in a cabin similar to this one while he was a slave on a plantation.

Work and School

Booker's family was poor. He had to work with his stepfather in the salt mines. A salt mine is a tunnel where people dig for salt. Booker did not want to work there. He wanted to go to school.

Booker could only attend school if he kept working. He worked in the mine from 4 A.M. until 9 A.M. He went to school until 3 P.M. Then, he went back to work for two more hours. Soon, he had to quit school to work longer hours.

Booker heard about a school for African Americans. In 1872, he left Malden to go to the Hampton Institute. This school was in Hampton, Virginia. He worked as a janitor to pay for school.

As a child, Booker always wanted to go to school.

Founder of Tuskegee Institute

Booker finished school at Hampton Institute in 1875. He taught at an African-American school for three years. But he returned to Hampton to teach night school.

Soon, Booker was asked to start a school in Tuskegee, Alabama. Students there needed a teacher and a school. Booker bought a run-down plantation in Tuskegee. He cleared the land and fixed the old buildings.

The school was called Tuskegee Institute. Over time, it expanded to cover 540 acres (216 hectares). More than 400 students lived on campus.

Teachers at the Tuskegeee Institute taught job skills to students.

Family Life

Booker met Fannie Smith in Malden. She was his childhood sweetheart. They married in 1882. Their daughter, Portia, was born one year later. Fannie died in 1884. Portia was one year old.

In 1885, Booker married Olivia Davidson. She was an assistant principal and a fund raiser at Tuskegee. Booker and Olivia had two sons. Their names were Booker Taliaferro Jr. and Ernest Davidson. Olivia died in 1889.

Booker met Margaret Murray during a college dinner party. He hired her to be a principal at Tuskegee. They enjoyed working together and married in 1893. Booker and Margaret did not have children.

Margaret Murray married Booker in 1893.

A Day at Tuskegee

Booker started a school based on his beliefs. He combined learning with hard work. He lived his life this way, too.

Booker rode around the school grounds on horseback. He watched teachers and students in their classrooms. He wrote letters asking people to support his school. He kept notes on all the teachers and workers. He sent letters of praise and fault.

Booker spent a lot of time running the school. He understood how important it was to know the students. He enjoyed teaching and talking with students. They called him Mr. B.T.

Booker rode his horse around the school grounds.

Ideas on Education

Booker thought education should lead to a job. He wanted students to learn thinking and job skills. Booker said that farming was as important as writing poetry.

Booker hired George Washington Carver to teach at his school. George was a great teacher and scientist. Booker and George shared many of the same goals in education.

Booker was also religious. However, he did not think religion belonged in the classroom. On Sundays at prayer services, he spoke to his students. He often asked his students if they were doing their best.

Booker thought education should lead to a job.

Spokesperson for African Americans

By 1895, Booker was a well-known African-American leader. He gave a speech in Atlanta, Georgia. This speech was called the Atlanta Compromise.

He believed that African Americans and white people could live separately. He felt African Americans should prove their equality through hard work.

W.E.B. Du Bois was another African-American leader. He questioned Booker's ideas. W.E.B. felt that African Americans should be educated beyond job training. He also felt that everyone should have the same rights. Both W.E.B. and Booker were well-respected leaders.

Booker spoke to crowds about his beliefs.

National Leader

Booker told others about his beliefs. He helped raise money to keep the school going. He traveled and met a lot of people. He told others about the success of his school.

Harvard University respected Booker for his leadership and work in education. The school gave him an honorary master's degree. A master's degree is awarded to people for study after college.

Booker also believed that African Americans should have well-paying jobs. He organized the National Negro Business League. In 1901, he wrote a book called *Up From Slavery*. Booker T. Washington died at his home in Tuskegee on November 14, 1915.

Booker died at his home in Tuskegee in 1915.

Words from Booker T. Washington

"Great men cultivate love, . . . only little men cherish a spirit of hatred."

From the book about Booker T. Washington's life, *Up from Slavery*, 1901.

"Learn to dignify and glorify common labor and put brains and skill into common occupations of life."

From the book about Booker T. Washington's life, *Up from Slavery*, 1901.

"More and more, we must learn to think not in terms of race or color or language or religion or political boundaries, but in terms of humanity."

From a speech at the Atlanta Convention in 1894.

Important Dates in Booker T. Washington's Life

1856—Born in Hales Ford, Virginia

1863—A U.S. law was signed that frees slaves

1865—Family moves to Malden, Virginia

1866—Leaves school to work in the salt mines

1872—Enters Hampton Institute in Hampton, Virginia

1875—Graduates from Hampton Institute

1879—Begins teaching at Hampton Institute

1881—Opens Tuskegee Institute in Alabama

1895—Gives a famous speech in Atlanta, Georgia

1900—Starts the National Negro Business League

1901—Writes his book, *Up From Slavery*

1915—Dies at Tuskegee on November 14

Words to Know

agriculture (AG-ruh-kul-chur)—the science of farming

Atlanta Compromise (at-LAN-ta KOM-pro-mize)—a famous speech given by Booker T. Washington in 1895

plantation (plan-TAY-shuhn)—a large farm

salt mine (SAWLT MINE)—a tunnel where people dig up salt

spokesperson (SPOKEZ-pur-suhn)—a person who speaks out for a group of people

Read More

Glieter, Jan and Kathleen Thompson. *Booker T. Washington.* Austin, Texas: Raintree Steck-Vaughn, 1987.

McKissack, Patricia and Frederick McKissack. *Booker T. Washington: Leader and Educator.* Hillside, N.J.: Enslow Publishers, 1992.

McKissack, Patricia and Frederick McKissack. *The Story of Booker T. Washington.* Chicago: Children's Press, 1991.

Roberts, Jack L. *Booker T. Washington: Educator and Leader.* Brookfield, Conn.: Millbrook Press, 1994.

Useful Addresses

Booker T. Washington Collection
Oakland Museum History Dept.
1000 Oak Street
Oakland, CA 94607

Tuskegee University Archives
c/o Library
Tuskegee, AL 36088

Internet Sites

Booker T. Washington
http://marink12.ca.us/~parkweb/BookerTC.html
African-American Literature: Booker T. Washington
http://gopher.lib.virginia.edu/exhibits/rec_acq/history/btw.html

Index